D.A.R.E DETECTIVES

THE MYSTERY ON LOVETT LANE

ROBIN GILLINGHAM

ISBN: 979-8-88768-003-3

CONTENTS

INTRODUCTION

In this book, the kids of Lovett Lane welcome a new family to their street.

They meet these new people. They help with their bags. They also help with all the large boxes.

There are large boxes with numbers on them.

The numbers are long and seem strange.

None of the kids from Lovett Lane understands what they mean.

1

There are also little bags of all colors. Many have shapes and lines. The other bags are just plain.

The kids who helped them move in agreed that there must be over seven hundred little bags.

What could be in those large boxes?

Why did one family need so many little bags of the same thing?

Along with this, the kids wondered what the funny smell was.

All around the people and all over their new house, there was the same smell.

The smell wasn't one they had smelled before.

It was a mystery to all of them.

They had lots of questions about these new people.

They knew they had to find answers.

They choose to get the D.A.R.E. Detectives to help.

They speak with Don, Anna, Rita, and Ed, and the D.A.R.E Detectives get right onto the case.

With easy-to-read sentences and decodable words, readers will build fluency and feel successful, while still enjoying the suspense of the story.

CHAPTER 1.
Meet the D.A.R.E. Detectives

It's likely that you have met the type of kid who is good at solving cases with clues.

This type of person is called a private eye or a detective.

Well, there just happens to be four of these kids who live in a small town called Mayville.

They all like a good mystery.

One sunny afternoon, these four friends sat at their favorite picnic spot.

They were eating delicious fruit pies from the bakery down the road.

Don, the leader of the group, has a special way of getting tasty treats for free.

You see, his grandma owns the best bakery in the city.

She gives Don's family the leftovers every Monday, Wednesday, and Friday.

The rest of the days of the week, except Saturday, she gives them to the farmer who lives next to her.

He trades her two dozen eggs for tarts, cookies, pies, and cakes.

Because Saturday is when most people come into shop, there are no leftovers then.

Another member of the team is Anna.

She lives in the last house on the street, and she is the one who likes to make everyone happy.

Anna likes to draw and paint, so she is always creating lovely art to give as gifts to her friends.

Her bedroom walls are covered in paintings, drawings, and photos.

Some pictures are close-ups of butterflies and other bugs.

Others are of flowers, gardens, and sunsets.

Anna loves nature.

But when she paints, she doesn't paint bugs and flowers and things like that.

She likes to paint sailboats and big ships.

Her mom has framed Anna's best sailboat painting, and it is on the wall in their dining room.

The one who thinks in unusual ways from all the rest of the group is Rita.

She uses her love for science to help her find the answers to most things.

One time, she made drinking water out of rainwater.

Another time, she built an outside oven out of wire and tin foil.

That thing really cooked food too!

The last member of the group is Ed.

He mostly likes riding his bike, playing ball, and swimming.

I guess you could say he is a big sports fan.

He wins the hardest worker award every year in most of the sports at school.

He is a fast thinker, and he likes to have things planned out.

The main problem with Ed is getting him to put a bat and ball down long enough to do anything else.

He is a good friend and helpful but extremely focused on being the best at everything.

Altogether, the four friends get along well.

They all have different ideas, they work well as a team, and they are all kind to each other.

Each one plays their own role in the detective group.

Because of their names, friendship, and skills; they gave their group its very own special name.

They call themselves the D.A.R.E. Detectives.

"D" is for Don, "A" is for Anna, "R" is for Rita, and "E" is for Ed.

After they came up with a name, they made posters to hang around town so people could call on them for help.

Now, they get calls at least once a week for a job.

One time, they had to find a lost kitten.

Another day, they searched all morning for a missing wallet.

But their favorite job was the case of the missing birthday present!

Once they found out the little brother hid it in the treehouse out back, the mom was so grateful and asked them to stay for the party.

After all, the party just wouldn't have been the same if the present hadn't been found.

The **D.A.R.E** actually came to find out that the little brother was just trying to keep it safe from an extra sneaky big brother.

For those who like a little mystery in life, being a detective is the perfect job.

Not only do you get to hunt, search, and look for clues while on a case, you have the absolute best of fun while doing it.

CHAPTER 2.

Moving In

It was a hot Thursday afternoon, and the **D.A.R.E.** detectives were drinking lemonade and swimming in Ed's backyard pool.

Just as Ed had the group eyeing his almost perfect dive, Anna's phone rang.

It was her mom.

She wanted to check on the kids and see if any of them might know who was moving into the old house on Lovett Lane.

For about five years now, a blue house had stood empty on that street.

Everyone always wondered when someone would buy it.

Some said it was haunted, and others said strange noises came from it deep in the night.

Once, Don and his older brother tried to explore it.

They got close enough to see in the windows, but it looked like they were all covered with old sheets.

Don said they also described a strange smell around the house.

Another time, Rita and her cousins snuck around to the back where there was a big grassy area.

It looked like there had been a garden there in the past.

17

They also saw an old black fence that was broken in some places.

After that, they noticed that, above one of the doors, there was a strange sign that said, "This door isn't safe. Don't use it."

That scared Rita and her cousins, and they left the house right away!

If the house was truly filled with ghosts, no one really knew it as it seemed like each time someone got close to finding out more about it, something scared them away.

After sitting there so long with no family to take care of it, even if it wasn't haunted, it sure did look like it!

When Anna got off the phone with her mother, she told the gang that the day had finally come.

Someone was moving into that creepy house on Lovett Lane.

At that moment, the kids all got big eyes and wide mouths.

At first, there was silence.

Then they all had many things to say.

The four detectives lived in the same area as the house, but not all on the same road.

They were all able to walk to it - or run away from it quickly... whichever was needed!

They all agreed that the new family must be from far away.

After all, anyone who lived anywhere near their town didn't want to have anything to do with living in that house!

Once they found out about the new people moving in, the D.A.R.E Detectives wondered what may happen next.

They wanted to be sneaky, but they knew that wasn't the kindest choice to make.

So, they decided to hang back, keep their distance, and see what new adventures were about to take place.

CHAPTER 3.

Getting to Know the New Ones

The next day began quietly as the new family pulled into the driveway of the blue house.

With shutters falling off and a few windows broken, it did look like it just might fall apart at any second.

There were cracks in the porch, chipped pieces off the stairs to the front door, and the trees out front needed lots of love and care.

If you think about it, though, maybe the house wouldn't really be that bad on the inside?

With the sheets hanging in every window, everyone was left to wonder.

Only two houses down was a lovely white house with a beautiful garden.

It had pretty rose bushes, two nice cars in the carport, and plants all along its walls.

Inside lived a nine-year-old girl named Mary.

She watched with wonder as she saw the family step out of their van and walk to the front of the house.

They each took a bag and sat it on the front steps.

The two back doors of the red van were left open, and another car pulled up beside it.

Two teenagers got out with handfuls of little bags.

They walked to the side door of the house and went inside.

As Mary watched, she decided she had to know more.

She walked to the dining room window, but she still couldn't see everything.

After looking for a bit longer, Mary began to worry that she would be seen.

So, she made up her mind to contact the D.A.R.E. Detective group.

Mary knew the four kids from school, and she went to art class with Anna.

She admired Anna's paintings and pictures.

Mary was a little younger than her, but the two girls had a lot in common.

The night of the art show downtown, Mary and Anna had set up their work side-by-side for everyone to see.

Their art class put on an art display each year.

In spring, the teacher always got in contact with a shop from the area, and they set up a deal to display the kids' art.

For a few weeks, the townspeople could admire the students' work and talent.

Also, last summer, Mary's mother babysat for Ed's little brother.

Mary had helped with the baby and learned she liked babysitting.

Ed's brother was almost one year old and was so much fun to play with.

A couple of times when the baby was picked up in the afternoons, Ed would come in with his mother to help with all the baby's items.

He seemed nice, but Mary never really had a chance to talk to him much.

As far as the other two members of the D.A.R.E. Detective group, Rita and

Don, she had only seen them at school and around town.

They were always nice to her, but she really didn't know much about them.

They were a grade above her, and their lunch times and outside times were not the same.

Since she knew Anna the best, Mary planned with her mom to call and see if Anna could come for a visit the next day after school.

Both mothers were fine with that, and by 4:00 p.m. the next day, Anna and Mary were on the lookout.

Mary explained everything to Anna.

She told her about the van, the car, and the two teenagers.

She told her about the constant strange feeling she had every time she saw one of them enter or leave the house.

Anna was excited to hear all the details and told Mary she would let her friends know what was going on.

She said she would tell Mary their plan in the coming days and asked if they might use Mary's house as a stakeout if they needed it.

Mary's house was built on a large hill, and she was able to see a lot of what happened on her street and the ones nearby.

In the moonlight after dark, she could still see the backyard well.

If any secret things were going to be happening after the sun goes down, they were sure to see them as well.

Along with those good views of the house, Mary had a treehouse from which you could see everything for miles, it seemed.

Also, down below the garden, there was a rock wall about four feet tall that would be quite easy to hide behind.

They could probably see a lot going on by hiding behind it.

Mary also mentioned that, from the attic window, it was possible to see all the way around the side of the house.

This was where the broken fence was, where an old garden seemed to have grown.

Of all the places near the spooky house, Mary's home on the hill was the best place to get a good view.

Anna said goodbye to Mary.

She left after thanking Mary's mother for the extra good milk and cookies she had served during her visit.

She was super excited to tell her friends all the details!

CHAPTER 4.

Helping Mrs. Crane

Anna quickly ran home and made a plan to meet with the other detectives at 8:00 a.m. sharp the next morning to begin the mission.

She explained that this case would take a few extra steps.

Before they could start looking for clues, they had to get to know the family better.

But, before they could do that, there would need to be some spying to do first.

At 8:00 a.m. on the dot the next day, the detectives met up at Mary's house.

They decided it was the best place to set up camp since she lived closer to the house than any of them.

Lovett Lane was full of nice homes.

Some had pools, some were small houses with gardens, and others had cool things like treehouses.

They all made sure Mary knew they were grateful for the use of her treehouse.

They decided when they spoke of meeting back at the treehouse, they would call it their "landing pad" as a code.

The words "landing pad" mean a place where you gather often.

Just like every other morning, Lovett Lane was calm and quiet.

Birds were flying overhead.

People were leaving for work, and some were having coffee on their porch.

It really was a nice place, so the family moving in really needed to fit in.

Mary's mom and a few other ladies from the area were planning to do a welcome visit and take cookies over the next day.

They wanted to give them a day or so to let them get settled.

As the detectives watched from the treehouse, everything seemed calm at the old blue house... so far.

After about **10** minutes of nothing, one of them finally came out of the front door and walked over to the red van.

They unloaded boxes, boxes, and more boxes.

Then they sat them all by the side door and went inside.

Afterwards, a black car pulled up with windows so dark, you couldn't see through them at all.

Four men in black suits, sunglasses, and black hats walked to the front door.

When they knocked, no one answered.

The **D.A.R.E.** Detective group knew the teenage kids who had just gotten boxes from the red van were inside the house.

So, the question was, why weren't they answering the door?

That made the gang wonder.

Were they scared of the people at the door, or was it because they were simply strangers?

After ringing the doorbell and knocking a few times, the four men got into the long, black car and drove away very slowly.

As the group talked about what all of that may have meant, they noticed the black car drive past down the street twice more.

Again, the black car stopped, and the men looked at all the big boxes the kids had sat down a while before.

They seemed to be looking for a certain one, but who knew for what reason.

They left the boxes as they were, hopped in the car, and sped off again.

Right after, a big moving truck came rolling into the drive.

The man driving immediately got out and ran to check the boxes.

He seemed overly concerned at first but became calmer after he looked through all the boxes.

A few seconds later, a lady came out of the front door, talked to the man for a while, and then he left.

She began to try and get the large boxes in the house on her own.

There was a side door that they were sitting closest to, so she slid them toward that door.

She seemed to be having a hard time, so the group decided that this would be a great time to meet her.

As the four children walked up the drive, the lady smiled and waved hello.

She said her name was Mrs. Crane, and she was happy to meet the kids.

So, they offered to help her with the big boxes, she seemed even happier they were there.

She was grateful for the help and offered the kids a cold bottle of water.

Having not completely moved in yet, there were not many choices for snacks.

The kids had a look around the outside a little closer but didn't get to see much of the inside except for the kitchen.

There were what seemed like hundreds of tiny little bowls, all the same size, sitting on the floor, next to the cabinet.

There were towels, a few glasses, and two plates that looked to be clean.

She explained that they weren't going to get all their belongings for a few more days.

She told the kids that anytime they wanted to come over, she would like their help.

Plus, she promised to have better snacks for next time as well!

CHAPTER 5.

What Could It Be?

The gang gathered back at the landing pad after the visit to Mrs. Crane's house.

They could only think that her husband was one of the men they saw earlier in the driveway.

They also agreed that the kids they saw in the van earlier were their children.

From what they talked about, there weren't too many strange things going on, but there were some concerns for sure.

As time passed over the rest of that week, Mary noticed several things.

She saw that, at night, the teenage kids would sometimes run a short way down the street whistling and screaming out strange words.

She couldn't understand what they were saying, but the whole thing was crazy.

She also noticed that the man they thought was the husband, Mr. Crane, would leave and only come home every other night.

He didn't come home every night as most dads would.

So, after watching and waiting, Mary and the D.A.R.E. Detectives decided it was time to venture back into the house.

They had to see more.

They just had to find out what was going on.

After a whole week of living there, not one stick had been picked up from the yard.

There wasn't one plant pot that sat up in the right way.

There wasn't one outside sign that anyone had moved into that old, creepy place.

The van and the car were proof someone was coming and going, but what was really going on there?

Late that evening, the four detectives made a trip to visit Mrs. Crane.

They hoped that when they rang the doorbell she would answer.

On the day that Mary's mom and her friends from the area had gone over to welcome the new family and take them cookies, no one had even come to the door!

So, they'd left the cookies and a card sitting on the chair next to the door.

However, that evening when the kids rang the bell, Mr. and Mrs. Crane answered.

Both had smiles and Mrs. Crane said to her husband, "These are the four sweet kids I told you about that helped me with the boxes the other day."

He welcomed them into their home and thanked them for helping.

The kids stated that they wanted to see if the family may need a little extra help with boxes or anything.

Mrs. Crane jumped up right away and offered them a job helping to place tiny bags of what felt like corn or rice into plastic bins.

After the kids finished, they agreed there must have been 600-700 little bags.

As they sat in wonder about what those bags could have been, Mrs. Crane stepped in and offered them lemon cake and fresh orange juice.

That did sound good to the kids, and there was no way they were passing it up!

About the time they were served their treat, they heard a very loud noise coming from the backyard.

Mr. Crane seemed concerned, and one of the teenagers ran down the stairs quickly and out the back door.

As for Mrs. Crane, she was as calm as ever and never looked away. What was happening?

After dark is when these strange noises happened, and their kids seemed to go crazy.

This was surely a problem that was going to have to be investigated quickly.

CHAPTER 6.

Let's Get to Work

After the kids left the Crane's home that night, they agreed to meet back at Mary's treehouse first thing in the morning to discuss the happenings of the night.

The loud noise and the little bags had left them with many questions.

As the night passed and the sun rose, the kids all had breakfast and headed to Mary's.

They arrived with notebooks, spying glasses, flashlights, and walkie-talkies.

A plan was made to find answers as soon as possible.

If there was a reason to worry, they had to find out quickly.

People in the area didn't need to be in danger, and it was the detectives' job to fix the problem if there was one.

They split into two groups.

Don and Rita were partners and Ed was with Anna.

Don said it looked like Mrs. Crane had removed the sheets from all the windows.

So, they decided one group needed to try and look inside each one.

The other two kids could search inside the house.

Ed and Anna chose to look in all the windows, and Don and Rita would be inside.

It wouldn't be so hard to sneak around the outside of the house, but Don and Rita had to be more creative.

While the two outside used their notebooks to keep track of everything they could see in each window, the others found a way inside.

Rita knocked on the front door and Mr. Crane answered it.

She told him that she thought she may have lost her bracelet at their house the night before.

She said that she told Don about it, and he wanted to help her look for it.

They explained they had already looked at their houses, and the only thing they could think of was that it may have been lost there.

He invited the kids in to look for it.

The story about the bracelet wasn't true, of course, but the idea of using that story got them into the house.

As they pretended to look for it, they snapped pictures with their phones.

They got pictures of every room they had been in the night before, but they wanted to consider the rooms they hadn't entered as well.

So, Don started chatting to Mr. Crane about the shops and places to eat around the town.

As he did that, Rita took the chance to visit all the rooms and snap pictures, except one.

The only room she couldn't get into had a locked door.

The lights didn't seem to be on, but she could feel cool air coming from under it.

Once she realized she wasn't going to get in, she went back to Don.

It seemed like she had been gone forever, but it only took a few minutes.

When Rita returned, she said she hadn't found the bracelet, and thanked Mr. Crane for allowing them to look for it.

She and Don said goodbye and left out the same door they came in.

As they stepped onto the grass, Ed and Anna were sneaking around from behind the house.

They both had things written down, and everybody was ready to compare their notes and pictures.

They quietly gathered back at the landing pad and pulled out everything they had.

Mary was excited to see all the notes they had taken.

Since it was right between breakfast and lunch, Mary thought the gang could use a snack.

Before she went to join them, she made a tray of cheese and crackers and grabbed five juice boxes from the fridge.

When she arrived, Don helped her carry up the tray and Anna grabbed the juice so Mary could hold onto the ladder.

Right away, they got started talking about everything they found.

The pictures showed normal items in each room, and Rita said she didn't see anything strange except the one locked door.

Ed and Anna reported about the same thing.

With the sheets removed, you could see into all the rooms, but again, there was nothing strange.

So, they decided that the next step would be to find answers by spying and being sneaky.

After all, they were detectives, and they had to keep the town safe!

CHAPTER 7.
Hiding Out

With their plan ready, the gang went home and relaxed for the afternoon.

Anna began a new painting, Ed played basketball with his big brother, Don played video games, and Rita got back to work on an ongoing science project.

Mary stayed in the treehouse for a few hours reading a new book.

At times, she looked over at the house but saw nothing out of place.

As the evening went on, the sun then set, the crickets started their loud chirping, and the frogs began to croak.

Ed went over his part for the next day.

He was going to keep an eye out for anyone pulling into the driveway or leaving.

He was also going to keep track of any cars that drove by slowly or looked odd.

Anna and Rita were going to sneak around the back and see if they could find out anything about the strange noises that came from the house.

They knew being quiet was important, so instead of making any noise, they agreed to use signs and codes to talk to each other.

They had made up a system of speaking without words two years ago when they first formed the detective group.

Don went over his part as well.

He would stand near the window on the left side of the house.

When Anna was taking pictures of the inside of the house the day before, she did get one especially useful picture.

This picture showed that the window on the side where Don was to stand was near the locked door.

So, his job was to stand near the window and keep a look out to see if anyone ever opened the door.

Through the night, each one of them slept well, but they made sure they were ready to get up the next morning.

They were certain that answers would be found... no matter what!

After breakfast, they met at the landing pad at about 7:45 a.m.

To start, Don went over everyone's job and made sure they had what they needed.

They agreed to walk over separately in case anyone was watching.

To avoid being seen by the Crane family, each one snuck around the tall pecan tree in the front yard on the side without using the driveway.

As each kid got into their spying place and began their work, the strange noise they had heard coming from the house happened again.

Anna and Rita looked at each other because it seemed the noise was near them.

They looked for what could be making the noise but couldn't find anything.

They decided it must be coming from inside the house.

Don thought the noise was very near him as well, and Ed heard it but knew he couldn't leave his spot.

It didn't seem so loud to him.

Don's eyes were always on the window, but he saw nothing when the noise was made.

However, right after he heard it, one of the sons came to the locked door, opened it, and went inside.

In his hands, he held a few of those little bags the kids had helped unpack a few nights ago.

The noise happened again and again, and Don could tell it was coming from whatever was behind that locked door.

While the kids were there, they did find a few answers, but not what they needed.

Ed never saw strange cars coming and going, and no one ever left or came home.

Anna and Rita found that the smell was strongest in the backyard, and mostly on the right side near where the fence was broken.

In the area that looked like it used to be a nice garden, there was a pair of old boots, a small animal cage, and a few bowls stacked up.

There was also a shovel and a chair.

From that, the girls couldn't really come up with any reason the smell would be there or where it may be coming from.

As they sat and thought, the kids decided to take a break for the next day because Ed and his family had something special to go to.

They would be gone all day but be home sometime before dark.

So, it seemed best that they just take a day off from clue hunting.

73

CHAPTER 8.

Did You See That?

The next day started out fine, but Mary really did want to find out more answers.

She wasn't part of the **D.A.R.E.** Detective group, but she did want to try finding out some things on her own.

Since they were taking the day off, she took the chance to sneak over to the Crane's house and see things for herself.

It was early morning, and no one seemed to be moving around in the house much.

One of the teenage boys that lived there left every day around noon.

The kids assumed that one had a job because he never returned until after dark.

The other son worked in the yard sometimes, spent some time playing basketball, and sometimes just sat on the front porch.

He was the younger of the two.

Mary felt like she had a few hours to look around, so she slowly took her time around the entire area of the house.

She noticed that there were some gardening tools on the back porch.

She also saw an old shower curtain laying near the animal cage inside the fence.

Other than that, everything she noticed seemed to be exactly the same as what the kids had reported the day before.

Since she didn't find much, she went on home to relax for a bit.

She had piano lessons at **11:00** a.m.

After that, she had a dentist's visit.

Mary wasn't happy about the dentist's visit, but it was time for a six-month tooth cleaning.

She knew no matter what she did, she wasn't getting out of it.

This summer was going great so far, and she didn't want the dentist to change that.

But she decided not to think about that until it was time to go.

After spending some time reading, Mary's mom had her do a few chores.

Before she knew it, the time had come for her to head to piano lessons.

She made it through that fine, and as much as she didn't want to go, she made it through the dentist visit okay too.

Sometime around 8:30 p.m., Mary heard the strangest noises.

She noticed all the Crane family members outdoors.

Mrs. Crane was in her bathrobe, and from a distance, it looked like Mr. Crane had on his pajamas and slippers.

They were in the front while the two boys were running around the sides and back of the house.

What in the world could they be doing?

She called her friends right away and let them know what was going on.

Ed and his family were back home, so they all decided to meet at the landing pad as soon as they could.

Within 10 minutes, all the detectives were there with Mary watching the crazy things going on in the Crane's front yard.

After a few minutes of watching, the kids all had the same question.

They were all asking each other, "Did you see that?"

They all saw a small dash of darkness across the front yard with one of the Crane boys chasing after it.

It was, for sure, time to find out what was *really* going on!

CHAPTER 9.
Oh No!

The kids all looked at each other with big eyes!

They talked quickly and decided to run over and ask the Cranes if they needed help.

It looked like a strange situation, but it also looked as if maybe they could use a few extra people to help stop whatever was happening.

The streetlights gave off some light but not much. It was hard to see hardly anything from far away.

The closer the kids got to their yard they could clearly see Mrs. Crane in her robe.

They could also see they were correct when they guessed that her husband was in his pajamas.

Don asked Mrs. Crane if they could help, and she explained that their pet had gotten out and was loose.

She told Don that their pet was incredibly special to them, and he could tell Mrs. Crane was truly upset.

Right away, he went to Ed, Rita, and Anna.

He told them about the missing pet.

They agreed that Mrs. Crane looked upset.

Don explained she didn't tell him what kind of pet it was, only that she loved it very much.

So, before the kids could start looking for a missing animal, they had to find out what kind it was.

Rita chose to be the one to ask the family exactly what they were looking for.

The answer surprised the gang, and they all looked at each other with shocked faces when Rita told them.

She explained that they were looking for a raccoon!

While they all searched in the yard and around the house, some of the other people in the area came over to help as well.

Many had flashlights, others used the lights on their phone, and they all looked for Roxy, the raccoon.

While they were looking for the pet, the girls found out that the small cage in the backyard was for Roxy.

She used it when she needed to get some fresh air outside.

The area around her cage wasn't fixed up nice with flowers and pretty things because Roxy didn't care about all those things.

She was nocturnal and was only awake at night.

The strange noises that came from the house were Roxy when she wanted attention or a snack.

Her bed and toys were in the locked room in the house.

The family kept the door locked so no one would open it by mistake and wake up their sweet raccoon.

The daylight would make her wake up and then her sleeping times would be wrong.

If that happened, Roxy would be in a bad mood for a few days and would refuse to play or eat as much as she should!

As the kids looked for Roxy, they came across the strange smell in the backyard.

They went ahead and asked Mr. Crane about it, and he told them it was the Bradford Pear trees that grew in the backyard.

Rita and Anna looked at each other with understanding.

That explained why the smell was there before the family moved in.

People who lived around the house had always been aware of it but didn't know what caused it.

They also asked about the back door with the warning sign above it.

Mr. Crane explained that the people who had lived there before had put up that particular sign.

The reason was that the door would almost fall off if it was opened.

It needed repair, but no one had ever gotten around to fixing it.

The girls told Mr. Crane they were so sorry his pet was missing and promised him they would look until they found her.

As Ed and Don walked down Lovett Lane, they had a chance to talk to the Crane boys.

They found out they would both be at their school when it started back in a couple of months.

They also found out that the boys were genuinely nice and seemed like good people to live nearby.

As the night carried on, they also learned that Roxy had been with the family since she was born.

Mrs. Crane had taken care of her and fed her milk through a medicine dropper.

She had lived with the family for four years, and they all adored her.

Finally, around **10:15** p.m. that night, Mrs. Crane got Roxy back.

The gang had looked everywhere until they found her in a tree five houses away.

She had gotten away as she was being moved to her cage out back to get some fresh air.

Even though she had been with the family for so long and loved them too, she did run off from time to time.

That explained the other nights when they had seen strange things going on after dark around the Crane's house.

Once everything and everyone had calmed down, Mrs. Crane invited the kids over the next day to have homemade cherry pie.

She wanted to thank them for not giving up until they found Roxy.

All four of them quickly agreed to that and promised to come back about 10:00 a.m. the next morning.

CHAPTER 10.
Conclusion

The next morning, the gang all showed up at the Crane's house right on time.

Homemade cherry pie would be a great summertime snack, and they were all happy to enjoy it with friends.

Yes, the new family who had moved into the old, blue house on Lovett Lane had become their new friends!

Jacob and Steve, the two teenage boys were in the kitchen with the kids arrived, and they all started talking about Roxy.

As Mrs. Crane fixed the plates of pie, everyone found a place at the table.

She served ice-cold milk for them to drink and handed everyone a cloth napkin.

While eating, Mr. Crane got a phone call from his work.

The kids could hear him talking about flying out of the country and wondered what type of job he had.

As he talked, Mrs. Crane could tell the kids were interested and began to tell them what exactly their jobs were.

She explained that they were builders who chose how buildings would look on the outside.

She helped her husband make models of his drawings, and they stored them in large boxes.

They then flew on an airplane to show companies their ideas.

They would take the drawings and a large box that was labeled with a code number to match the drawing.

At that point, the kids understood the code numbers on the large boxes and how they must match each of Mr. Crane's ideas for his buildings.

After learning all these new things about the Crane family, the D.A.R.E.

detectives only had one question left that was unanswered.

So, they agreed to ask it before they left the house that day.

The very last question they had was about all the small bags they had unloaded the night they helped with the boxes.

The noises had been explained.

The smell and running around in the yard after dark had been explained.

The locked door and all the coded boxes had even been explained.

But they still wondered about those little bags!

Rita went ahead and asked Mrs. Crane about them as she helped her pick up the pie plates and put them in the sink.

What Mrs. Crane had to say was great.

She said that they were 'treat bags' for Roxy!

Sometimes, when she did tricks or behaved well, they would pick out three to four treat bags and let her pick which one she wanted.

They had different treats inside, and Roxy could smell what was in each bag.

Later, after they all told the family goodbye and thanked them for the pie, Rita filled the others in.

Everyone was so happy to know that those little bags were nothing more than treat bags for a family pet.

The D.A.R.E. detective group reported back to Mary that afternoon.

She, too, was super happy to learn that there was nothing strange about the new family across the street.

She thanked the detectives for their work, and they all agreed to stay in touch through the summer.

In fact, they did just that.

They swam at Ed's house, had lunch at the landing pad, and joined Rita for a science experiment in her backyard.

The friends also had picnics, went on walks, and played tag football in Don's front yard.

They also spent a lot of time planting a flower garden at Anna's.

They had such a fun summer, and the group of four became the group of five when they decided to make Mary a member of the D.A.R.E. Detectives!

Made in United States
Orlando, FL
21 October 2023

38012531R00059